"Give me a place to stand and I will move the Earth."

So boasted a great scientific genius more than 2,000 years ago.

Who was this genius? His name was Archimedes. The Greeks called him "Alpha" (α), meaning "First," or "Greatest." In an age without computers or calculators, without even pen and paper, he discovered many important scientific laws or principles. They include the Law of Buoyancy, the Law of the Lever, and many others. He led us through the great door of science. Today, in our complex modern world of airplanes, satellites, and submarines, his discoveries live on.

Not much was written about Archimedes during his lifetime. But many stories about him have been passed down through the ages. Some stories are funny; some are brilliant. Others are quite incredible, even fantastic. Yet when carefully pieced together, these story fragments, like the scattered bits of a jigsaw, give us many clues as to what kind of person Archimedes was.

Actually, the first man to set off in search of Archimedes was the Roman statesman and writer, Cicero. In 75 B.C. Cicero traveled to Archimedes' homeland, the island of Sicily.

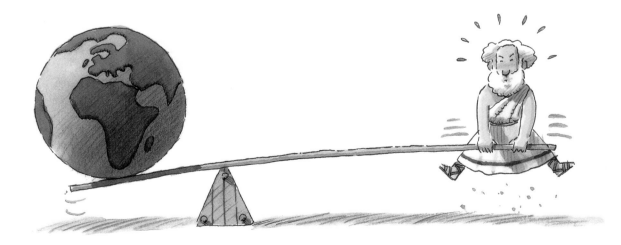

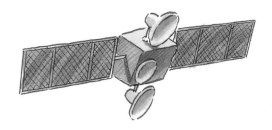

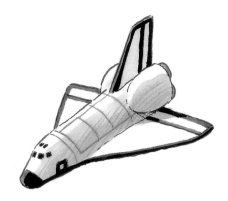

Mason Crest Publishers, Inc.
370 Reed Road
Broomall, Pennsylvania 19008
866-MCP-BOOK (toll free)

Illustrations copyright © 1999 Stefano Tartarotti
Published in association with Grimm Press Ltd., Taiwan

1 3 5 7 9 8 6 4 2

Library of Congress Cataloging-in-Publication Data:

on file at the Library of Congress.

ISBN 1-59084-152-2
ISBN 1-59084-133-6 (series)

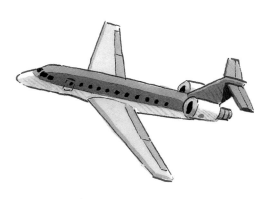

Great Names

ARCHIMEDES

Mason Crest Publishers

Philadelphia

THE SEARCH BEGINS

July 1 – Fine

Our boat entered the harbor slowly. The sky and the sea were crystal blue. The air was sweet with the fragrance of olives. Standing on deck and watching the passing ships, I was filled with excitement. I wanted to shout, "I'm here! I've arrived!"

This small island in the Mediterranean is a busy commercial port steeped in Greek culture, poetry, and music. Through the ages, Sicily has been a home to philosophers, artists, and scientists. It glitters eternally in the midst of the ocean.

I have been sent here by the Roman Emperor to serve as governor of Sicily. I couldn't be happier, for now I can begin my search for my hero: Archimedes.

Who was Archimedes? He was a scientific genius and a mathematical wizard. He is also a man who completely unnerved the great Roman navy! I've heard so many fascinating stories abut Archimedes, I simply have to retrace his steps and discover what he was like.

MARCVS TVLLIVS CICERO

ARCHIMEDES' BIRTHPLACE

August 1 – Fine

I have been here a month now, and I have to say, Sicily is the most beautiful Greek state I have seen.

Today I began an official visit to Syracuse, where Archimedes was born. Syracuse is a large port on Sicily's east coast, where the Asian, European, and African shipping routes come together. This perfect location makes Syracuse a flourishing trade center and the envy of its neighbors. Those more powerful neighbors have often attacked Sicily, causing the city to go through a continuing cycle of war and prosperity.

Early in its history, Syracuse was conquered and colonized by Greece. When the Greek Empire fell into decline, Syracuse became a small, independent nation. The Greeks left their mark, though. Today I can still see the Greek influence in the buildings, roads, clothes, and food. As I wander the narrow, winding lanes, it is easy to imagine Archimedes living here. I can picture him giving lectures in the marketplace, or holding deep discussions on the steps.

Note: Greek culture was the cradle of Western civilization. It produced many great thinkers. They included the astronomer Thales, the mathematician Pythagoras, and the philosophers Plato and Aristotle.

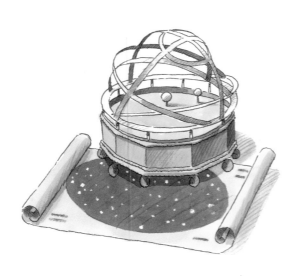

ARCHIMEDES BEGINS LIFE

September 10 – Hot and Sunny

I thought I would learn a lot about Archimedes once I got to Syracuse. So far I haven't, though, so I have ordered my soldiers to go out and make inquiries. Whatever they can find—a text, an invention, anything—will be of priceless value to me. Archimedes was born into an educated family. His father, Pheidias, was a noted astronomer. Pheidias spent his life studying the relationship between the earth, sun, and moon; and the distance between the stars.

Pheidias, like all fathers, greeted the birth of his son with great pleasure and hope. He chose for him the name Archimedes, meaning "great thinker." As soon as the boy was old enough, Pheidias hired the best teachers to instruct Archimedes in mathematics, science, literature, and philosophy. Pheidias himself taught Archimedes astronomy. I imagine what these lessons must have been like. As I gaze on the starry heavens arching brightly overhead, I think of Pheidias, hand in hand with his son, pointing out the constellations and teaching Archimedes their names.

THE EARLY YEARS

September 18 – Brilliant sunshine

It is hot. The sun has been shining every day this month. In heat like this, it's hard to think. So today, like everyone else, I headed to the seaside. The beach was crowded. The adults rested while the children built sandcastles, tossed sand, and played happily. But if Archimedes had been here, I am sure he would have been busy with his formulas.

Once Archimedes began his education, his intelligence was obvious. He loved mathematics and science. He adored Homer's epic poems and Aesop's fables. Sometimes the hardworking Archimedes became so wrapped up in his studies that he forgot to eat or sleep.

In those days, studying wasn't easy. Everything was written on the ground with a stick, or carved into a wax tablet with a knife. But Archimedes never tired of this. Once, when he was taking a bath, he began thinking of solutions to a tricky geometry problem. He had no way to write down his calculations, so he scratched them into his skin.

Later, Archimedes discovered quite by chance that the beach was a perfect natural "chalkboard." The sand was easy to write in and easy to erase. Throughout his life, whenever he had a difficult problem to solve, Archimedes would go to the beach and write his calculations over and again in the sand.

Among the happy crowd on the beach, was there anyone who knew that the footprints of a genius were once imprinted on that stretch of sand?

STUDY ABROAD

September 27 – Cloudy

No progress to report in the search for Archimedes. My governing of the city is going smoothly, though. I have decided to build an assembly in the town center, and to expand the port to attract more foreign ships to conduct trade. Each foreign ship that arrives here is like a window to the outside world, showing us new and exciting things.

Archimedes, too, was interested in the outside world. In his free time, he often went to the harbor to look around and ask questions. Someone once told him that beyond the sea was a country called Egypt. The capital of Egypt, Alexandria, was the world's most famous center of learning. It had a magnificent library with more than 700,000 books. Young students came from all over the world to be taught by Alexandria's great teachers, such as Euclid, the father of geometry. "What is it like at such a center of learning?" wondered Archimedes. He wanted nothing more than to learn. He did not have to wait long to find an answer to his question. None other than King Hieron helped send Archimedes to Alexandria. The young genius was just 11 years old! How must he have felt, all by himself in a strange land?

By the time Archimedes arrived in Egypt, Euclid was already dead. But Archimedes studied with Euclid's own pupil, who admired the intelligent young student very much. The years passed, and Archimedes grew. As he grew, his knowledge grew with him.

The Conch and the Screw

October 5 – Rain

Great news! The soldiers have found the machine Archimedes invented to pump water. It is called the Archimedes Screw. This marvelous invention improved the lives of millions of farmers; but few would have imagined that it was inspired by a simple conch shell.

Archimedes lived in Egypt for many years. Egypt is a dry country with little rain. In the dry season, people had to carry water to their fields by hand. Archimedes was upset to see people sweat and work so hard under the fierce summer sun. He determined to find a way to help them.

One day, Archimedes saw a conch shell. Its spiral shape gave him the idea of designing a machine along the same lines. This was the Archimedes Screw. The device is basically a hollow tube containing a large spiral screw. It is placed on an angle, with one end in the water. When the handle is turned, the spinning screw carries water quickly and easily along its blades and up through the tube.

Note: The modern world has many things that can be traced to the Archimedes Screw. They include propellers, spiral staircases, and screws.

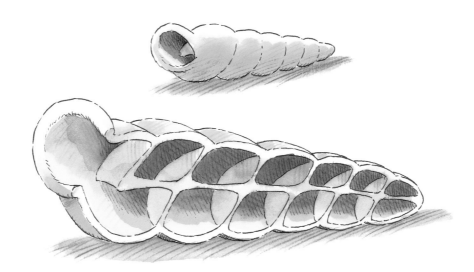

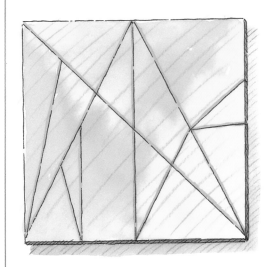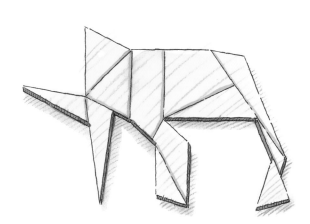

GEOMETRY
October 10 – Gray and wet

The search for Archimedes is finally beginning to bear fruit. Today a man who said he was the son of one of Archimedes' students visited me. The man brought many items that had belonged to the great teacher. The items included an Archimedes Planetarium and a game called the Archimedes Box. Looking at these treasures, I am filled with admiration for the exceptional thinker who made such great contributions to mathematics, physics, and astronomy.

Archimedes inherited the legacy of the great master, Euclid. Archimedes continued Euclid's work in geometry, such as investigating the shape, area, and volume of solids. One time, Archimedes even climbed a garden wall in order to get a better look at the shape of a window. He was chased away by the angry men of the household!

In time, Archimedes' achievements surpassed those of the great Euclid. Some even say Archimedes knew how to calculate the number of grains of sand on a beach! One of his greatest accomplishments involved the number known as pi (π), which is used to calculate the circumference, or outer size, of a circle. Archimedes proved that pi was a number between 3.1409 and 3.1429. Another accomplishment was proving that the ratio of the volume of a cube to the sphere it contained was 3:2. Archimedes was so proud of this discovery that he told his family to record it on his tombstone.

Pi (π): By Archimedes' time, the Greeks knew that the circumference of a circle was about three times its diameter. Archimedes took this further, and worked out a value close to the 3.1415926 we use today.

THE PROBLEM OF THE GOLD CROWN

October 25 – Cold winds

Today a Syracuse merchant brought me a gold crown that was dug up in an ancient Greek cemetery. Although it is very old, every one of its golden leaves gleams as brightly as ever. It brings to mind a funny story.

When Archimedes was 47, he returned to Syracuse and became an advisor to King Hieron. The king had ordered a gold crown to be made, but he suspected that the goldsmith had stolen some of the gold and used silver in its place. The king asked Archimedes to find a way to test the crown without damaging it. This was a difficult problem even for Archimedes. He spent much time trying to think of a solution.

The answer came while Archimedes was taking a bath at a public bathhouse. When he climbed into a bathtub full of water, Archimedes noticed the water spilling out onto the floor. Suddenly, he jumped out of the bath. Without even stopping to dress, he ran from the room, shouting, "Eureka! Eureka!" (meaning, "I have found it!"). The overflowing water had suggested to him the idea of displacement, where an object of a certain weight displaces a certain amount of water from a container. Archimedes now realized that in order to solve the king's problem, he needed to obtain a lump of pure gold that weighed as much as the crown. Archimedes knew that the lump of gold and the crown should displace equal amounts of water. They didn't. The thief was caught.

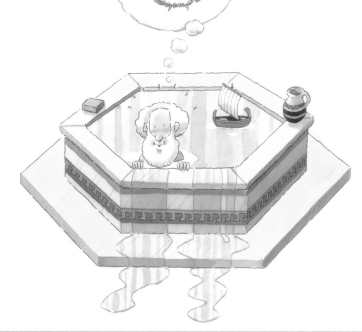

GIVE ME A PLACE TO STAND
November 2 – Rain clearing

Why is it possible to move a huge stone with a lever, but not without one? When Archimedes finished studying displacement, he turned his attention to another scientific riddle: the lever. Archimedes designed a piece of equipment something like a balance, with a horizontal pole and a moveable point of support, with which to conduct his experiments. He discovered that the force exerted by a pole increased or decreased depending on the position of the point of support. After much calculation, Archimedes discovered a law:

force × force applied = weight × weight applied

Archimedes wrote excitedly to the king: "Give me a place to stand, and I will move the Earth." At first, King Hieron II thought that Archimedes' long hours of research and experimentation had driven him mad; but Archimedes soon proved himself quite sane. Using his new Law of the Lever, he connected a series of complicated pulleys. When King Hieron gently turned the handle, he lowered a fully laden boat into the water below. The king was so amazed he was speechless.

ROME ATTACKS

December 10 – Crisp and clear

Today I went to inspect the harbor. I plan to build a new city wall to better protect the city against invasion from the sea. While I was there, I recalled that our great Roman navy suffered many defeats here, not because of any stone and cement wall, but through the genius of Archimedes.

When Rome was at war with Carthage, Syracuse was caught in the middle. Each side greedily wanted Syracuse. To protect itself, Syracuse had to bend with the wind, sometimes leaning toward Rome, other times, toward Carthage. When Hieron II died, his successor was murdered. Within Syracuse, civil war broke out between those who favored Rome and those who preferred Carthage. Eventually, Carthage won. An angry Rome sent its navy to attack. At the time, Archimedes was already an old man of 70. Still, he worked mightily to defend his homeland. He invented a number of clever weapons. One was a catapult, that rained stones down on the heads of the Romans. Another was a revolving crane. Amazingly, the crane could pick up a warship and turn it upside down, dumping warriors, weapons, and supplies onto the rocks or water below. Again and again, the Romans were turned back.

Catapult: Based on the Law of the Lever, a length of tendon is stretched tightly and then released. When it springs back, a rock is propelled out at great speed.

Revolving crane: No detailed design information exists about this machine. It probably combined a series of pulleys and levers, making it possible to lift a heavy boat with little effort.

The heat of the sun: Once, Roman warships surrounded Syracuse. Things looked very bad indeed for the city. Archimedes pieced together dozens of small mirrors to form a large hexagonal mirror that he hung on the city walls. The noon sun reflected off the mirrors and onto the Roman ships. The heat sparked fires that destroyed the ships and their crew.

Archimedes caused the Romans to suffer many losses at Syracuse. The Roman commander Marcellus complained bitterly: "Archimedes is a mathematical devil. He has scared the life out of our brave Roman soldiers." The Roman troops were so unnerved that when a branch appeared above the city wall, they took off in fright, thinking this was the beginning of some new trick from Archimedes.

AN UNTIMELY DEATH

December 12 – Cold drizzle

As we learn more and more about Archimedes, my appreciation of his genius and his greatness grows. I am profoundly impressed by his lifelong investigations of scientific principles, by his love of science, and by his contributions to his country.

In the last few days, I have found some of his handwritten manuscripts. I have sorted them out and passed them on for translation. I do this to show my personal respect for the man, and to apologize to him on behalf of all Romans. For Archimedes was murdered by a brutish Roman soldier.

After several defeats, the Roman army called off its attacks on Syracuse. Instead, it surrounded the city with a blockade. The blockade lasted for two years before the Romans finally captured the city. In the final attack, the Roman soldiers let loose all their anger and hatred. They behaved like wild animals, burning, looting, and killing. They turned Syracuse into a living hell. The commander Marcellus, though, gave strict orders that Archimedes was not to be harmed.

The soldiers found the old scholar on the beach, hard at work on a geometry problem. He had no idea what had been happening. When the soldiers demanded that Archimedes go with them, he cried angrily, "Get away! Don't wreck my diagram!" One of the soldiers pulled out his sword and waved it at Archimedes. Only then did the great thinker realize that this was the enemy. He pleaded for more time to finish his geometry problem. The soldiers cut him down on the spot. Archimedes died at age 75, with his final calculations left incomplete in the sand.

THE FORGOTTEN TOMB

December 24 – Clear skies

I am now approaching the end of my search for Archimedes. The most important thing left was to find his tomb. History records it as being in Syracuse. After all these years, though, the locals knew nothing about it; indeed, they even denied it existed. I sent my soldiers out again; but time after time, they came back with nothing. Yet I was determined. I would not let Archimedes' glory sleep forever in some deserted, overgrown corner! I took up the search myself, and swore to continue it for as long as there was hope.

My horsemen and I visited cemetery after cemetery. We examined every brush- and scrub-covered grave. Our disappointment grew with each failure. Just when all seemed lost, I noticed a broken column peeking above the scrub. Atop the column sat a sphere and a cube. Could this be the tombstone Archimedes had requested in his will? Excitedly, I ordered the area to be cleared.

A large part of the headstone was damaged by exposure to wind, rain, and sun. Still, I could make out a few lines of verse.

"Archimedes, I have found you at last!" I cried. I walked over and stroked the mottled stone. "In this forgotten graveyard you have slept as a forgotten genius, a neglected giant. I will restore you to your rightful glory, for now and ever more."

EPILOGUE

Cicero ordered Archimedes' tomb to be restored so that future generations could know his glory and his greatness. Today, even if we can't all go to Sicily and visit Archimedes' tomb, we can find traces of him in the things that surround us.

They are found in such things as seesaws, builders' screws, and submarines. These and many more items have been developed through discoveries made by Archimedes. They are his legacy to the world.